# KILLER BEES

## BY LISA OWINGS

BELLWETHER MEDIA • MINNEAPOLIS, MN

**Jump into the cockpit and take flight with Pilot books. Your journey will take you on high-energy adventures as you learn about all that is wild, weird, fascinating, and fun!**

This edition first published in 2013 by Bellwether Media, Inc.

No part of this publication may be reproduced in whole or in part without written permission of the publisher. For information regarding permission, write to Bellwether Media, Inc., Attention: Permissions Department, 5357 Penn Avenue South, Minneapolis, MN 55419.

Library of Congress Cataloging-in-Publication Data

Owings, Lisa.
   Killer bees / by Lisa Owings.
      pages cm. – (Pilot. Nature's deadliest)
   Includes bibliographical references and index.
   Audience: Ages 8-12.
   Summary: "Fascinating images accompany information about killer bees. The combination of high-interest subject matter and narrative text is intended for students in grades 3 through 7"–Provided by publisher.
   ISBN 978-1-60014-880-4 (hardcover : alk. paper)
   1. Africanized honeybee–Juvenile literature. 2. Bee attacks–Juvenile literature. I. Title.
   QL568.A6O95 2013
   595.79'915–dc23
                                        2012031234

Printed in the United States of America, North Mankato, MN.

# CONTENTS

Swarm! _____ 4

Stings and Other
    Deadly Things _____ 10

Killer Bee Attacks _____ 18

Glossary _____ 22

To Learn More _____ 23

Index _____ 24

# Swarm!

Fifteen-year-old Romeo Reyes Jr. of Tucson, Arizona was ready to spend the rest of his Sunday afternoon relaxing. He and his father, brother, and cousin had been working hard to clean up their backyard. They were almost done for the day when Romeo's father decided to tackle one more project.

Mr. Reyes wanted to get rid of an old dresser that had been sitting in the yard for years. The dresser was wedged between a shed and a concrete wall. Mr. Reyes climbed into the tight spot. He didn't hear the faint buzzing as he got closer. He had no idea a large **colony** of killer bees was preparing to defend their home.

## Terror in Arizona

Killer bees first appeared in Arizona in 1993. They have since taken over every hive in the state.

Mr. Reyes opened the top drawer of the dresser. Within seconds, a **swarm** of killer bees was attacking his face. They plunged their stingers deep into his skin. Painful bumps spread across his body. Mr. Reyes was desperate to get away. He ran to the fence surrounding the yard and scrambled over it. Then he fell into the alley on the other side.

Romeo saw his father fall and rushed to help him. That's when he saw the deadly swarm. He tried to swat the bees away from his father. That only made them angrier. The **lethal** insects had found a new victim.

The furious bees swarmed around Romeo's head. The buzzing was deafening. Then came the blinding pain. Romeo could feel his face swell up as dozens of stingers pierced his skin. He and his father bolted for their swimming pool, but the gate was locked. Mr. Reyes made a run for the house. Romeo hung back. He didn't want the swarm to follow him inside.

## Headed for Trouble

**Killer bees often go straight for their victim's face or head. Romeo Reyes learned this the painful way. Most of the bee stings were on his scalp.**

Thinking fast, Romeo's brother grabbed a hose and sprayed the bees off Romeo. The brothers knew they didn't have long before the bees dried off and attacked again. Luckily, another family member called 911. Romeo was rushed to the hospital along with his brother and cousin. Doctors carefully removed 150 stingers from Romeo's swollen body. Romeo went home the next day.

## After the Attack

The Tucson Fire Department sprayed the hive in Romeo's yard with poison to kill the bees. The hive was large enough to fill the whole dresser.

# Stings and Other Deadly Things

In the 1950s, Brazilian scientists were looking for ways to make the country's honeybees more productive. The honeybees in Brazil had been brought over from Europe. They couldn't **pollinate** many crops or produce much honey in Brazil's **tropical** climate. So the scientists brought bees over from Africa. African bees thrived in a climate similar to Brazil's. The scientists bred the African honeybees with some of their European honeybees. The offspring were called Africanized honeybees.

## Tricky Buzzness

It's difficult to tell the difference between Africanized and European honeybees. Africanized bees are just a tiny bit smaller. They are also more aggressive, and they move to new nests more often. The only way to tell the difference for sure is by doing a scientific test.

European honeybee

Africanized honeybee

**North America**

Africanized honeybee territory = ▢

N
W · E
S

**South America**

paper clip

**Africanized honeybee**

## The Sting of Death
**Killer bees have been blamed for more than 1,000 human deaths since they arrived in the Americas.**

Africanized honeybees seemed to do a better job in Brazil than European bees. However, they were also much more **aggressive**. In 1957, some of the Africanized honeybees escaped into the wild. They spread quickly throughout South America and took over the hives of European bees. The bees reached Mexico in the 1980s and entered the United States in 1990. They have been spreading ever since.

African honeybees had to be fierce to survive Africa's climate and predators. They passed this tough nature on to their Africanized offspring. That's why killer bees will do anything to defend their hive. They attack even the smallest threats. They react much faster than European bees and sometimes chase their victims for more than a quarter mile (0.4 kilometers).

Killer bees do not have an especially powerful sting. What makes them so deadly is that they may attack in groups more than ten times larger than other bees. Thousands of killer bees will attack a single victim. For those **allergic** to bee **venom**, just one sting can be deadly. Hundreds of stings from Africanized bees could kill just about anyone.

## Lethal Dose

**A lethal dose of bee venom is about 10 stings per pound (22 stings per kilogram) of body weight. A deadly dose may be far lower for children and unhealthy or allergic adults.**

## The Honeybee Hive

Each honeybee hive has a queen bee, male drones, and female workers. The queen mates with the drones and lays eggs. The workers feed the young. They also build and defend the hive. Only worker bees leave the hive to respond to threats.

venom pouch ———

A killer bee's stinger is its only weapon. **Barbs** on the stinger help it stick deep in the victim's skin. The stinger is attached to a venom pouch inside the bee's **abdomen**. When a killer bee stings, special muscles push venom through the stinger. When the bee flies away, the venom pouch rips out. The bee dies within minutes. But the venom keeps pumping into the victim.

Killer bee venom causes sharp pain. The area around the sting becomes red and swollen. Those who receive enough stings or are allergic can have a severe reaction. They can go into **anaphylactic shock**. People who react to bee venom this way can die within one hour.

## Anaphylactic Shock Symptoms

- difficulty breathing
- difficulty swallowing
- nausea or vomiting
- stomach cramps
- dizziness
- red skin or rashes

15

A honeybee's sting triggers the release of an alarm scent. The alarm scent warns other bees of a threat to the hive. It also marks the victim so the bees can easily find and attack the threat. Bees pick up this scent with their **antennae**. Africanized bees produce more of the alarm scent than European bees. They are also more sensitive to it. Even if the scent is very faint, they immediately rush to defend their home.

Killer bees also use their eyes to guard against threats. All bees have five eyes. Their vision is poor, but they can detect even the slightest movement. This makes it easy for them to land on swaying flowers. It also makes them experts at attacking moving targets.

antennae

## Going Bananas

**Survivors of killer bee attacks say the bees' alarm scent smells like bananas.**

# How Killer Bees Spread

## Swarming

A queen bee leaves her hive with about half of its bees to form a new hive. A new queen takes over the old hive.

## Afterswarming

A new queen leaves a hive with some of its bees after the old queen has left. She leaves because there are still too many bees in the hive after the first swarm.

## Absconding

A whole colony of bees leaves its hive to find a new one. Bees do this when they face threats or need to find food.

## Invading

A group of Africanized honeybees takes over a hive occupied by European honeybees.

# Killer Bee Attacks

Killer bees attack when defending their hives or themselves. That means you will not be a victim unless they see you as a threat. Keep a close watch for bee activity near your home and when outdoors. To prevent an attack, steer clear of all honeybee hives and never swat at bees.

If you find a hive, call pest control to have it safely removed. Stay at least 50 feet (15 meters) away. If you must go closer, move slowly and quietly. Loud noises and quick movements anger bees. If you disturb a hive by accident, run and find shelter as fast as you can. Once you are safe, remove any stingers. Seek medical help if your stings are severe or you have an allergic reaction.

## Beware the Water

You might be tempted to jump in water to get away from attacking bees. Don't do it! The bees will wait for you to come up for air and then attack.

# Bee Sting First Aid

1. Scrape stingers out with a fingernail or the edge of a credit card. Don't use tweezers. They can squeeze more venom into your body.

2. Wash stings with soap and water.

3. Use cold packs to help reduce pain and swelling.

## Where to Look for Hives

- under rooftop edges
- inside small structures such as electrical boxes or birdhouses
- in furniture or appliances left outside
- in or near garages or sheds
- within wood piles
- inside hollow trees
- on exposed branches

We would be in trouble without the honeybee's hard work. When honeybees pollinate, they help plants reproduce. Our food crops grow as a result of bee pollination. Africanized bees, however, are not the helpers that other honeybees are. They do not work well in certain climates. As they spread through new regions, they also threaten the bees that we need to live.

The number of killer bees in the wild increases every day. Scientists are researching ways to keep them from attacking more people and wiping out other bee populations. But for now, killer bees are on the loose. Tread lightly and beware of buzzing!

# Glossary

**abdomen**—the rear section of an insect's body

**aggressive**—violent or threatening

**allergic**—having a negative physical reaction to a substance

**anaphylactic shock**—a severe and often deadly reaction to a substance such as bee venom

**antennae**—feelers on the head of an insect; honeybees use their antennae to smell.

**barbs**—sharp spikes; the barbs on a honeybee's stinger prevent the stinger from falling out of the victim's skin.

**colony**—a group of bees that live and work together

**lethal**—deadly

**pollinate**—to help plants reproduce by moving pollen from one plant to another

**swarm**—a large group of insects that move together

**tropical**—part of the tropics; the tropics is a hot, rainy region near the equator.

**venom**—poison produced by some insects, snakes, and other animals

# To Learn More

## At the Library

Buchmann, Stephen L. *Honey Bees: Letters from the Hive*. New York, N.Y.: Delacorte Press, 2010.

Hamilton, Sue. *Swarmed By Bees*. Edina, Minn.: ABDO Pub. Co., 2010.

Rotner, Shelley, and Anne Woodhull. *The Buzz on Bees: Why Are They Disappearing?* New York, N.Y.: Holiday House, 2010.

## On the Web

Learning more about killer bees is as easy as 1, 2, 3.

1. Go to www.factsurfer.com.

2. Enter "killer bees" into the search box.

3. Click the "Surf" button and you will see a list of related Web sites.

With factsurfer.com, finding more information is just a click away.

# Index

African honeybees, 10, 12
alarm scent, 16
allergies, 12, 15, 18
Arizona, 4, 7
attack prevention, 18
barbs, 15
Brazil, 10, 11
climate, 10, 12, 20
colonies, 4, 17
deaths, 11, 12, 15
European honeybees, 10, 11,
    12, 16, 17
eyes, 16
first aid, 19
hives, 7, 9, 11, 12, 13, 16, 17,
    18, 20
pollination, 10, 20
population, 21
Reyes, Romeo, 4, 7, 8, 9
size, 10, 11

spreading, 11, 17, 20
stingers, 7, 8, 9, 15, 18, 19
swarms, 7, 8, 12, 17
symptoms, 15, 19
territory, 7, 11, 20
venom, 12, 15, 19
venom pouch, 14, 15

The images in this book are reproduced through the courtesy of: Peter Waters, front cover,
pp. 8-9; sergey23, p. 5; Ryan McVay/Getty Images, p. 6; Kent Wood / CMSP "CMSP
Biology"/Newscom, p. 10; Andrey Burmakin, p. 11; Steven Russell Smith Photos, p. 13;
Dr. Jeremy Burgess/Photo Researchers, Inc., p. 14; Antagain, p. 16; Zsschreiner, pp. 17,
19; Tony Campbell, p. 20; alle, p. 21.